Helping Children See Jesus

ISBN: 978-1-933206-90-5

DEPTHS OF GRACE
The Life of John Newton

Author: Thomas Luttmann
Illustrator/Computer Graphic Artist: Zachary Franzen
Proofreaders: Audrey Brubaker, Barry and Jean Keiser, Sharon Neal, Elinor Rogers
Typesetting and Layout: Patricia Pope

© 2016 Bible Visuals International
PO Box 153, Akron, PA 17501-0153
Phone: (717) 859-1131
www.biblevisuals.org

DEPTHS OF GRACE
The Life of John Newton

Author: Thomas Luttmann

ONLINE HELPS: Free key word sheets are available for this story. Visit our online store at shop.biblevisuals.org and search for item #K5092.

Memory Verse:

We then, as workers together with Him, beseech you also
that ye receive not the grace of God in vain . . .
behold, now is the accepted time;
behold, now is the day of salvation.
(2 Corinthians 6:1, 2)

Chapter 1

Grace Unknown

"What is God, John?" asked his mother.

John thought for a moment, then sat up in his chair and began. "God is a Spirit, infinite, eternal, and unchangeable, in his being, wisdom, power, holiness, justice, goodness and truth."

His mother continued. "Are there more Gods than one?"

"That one's easy, Mother. 'There is but one only, the living and true God.'"

"Very good, John. You'll have the Shorter Catechism memorized before you're six."

Each morning, John and his mother would review the Westminster Shorter Catechism, a series of 106 questions and answers used to teach John the basics of the Christian faith.

"What is the work of creation?" she continued.

"The work of creation is, God making all things of nothing, by the word of His power, in the space of six days, and all very good."

Before they could go any further, they were interrupted by his mother's coughs. She stood up and hurried to the other room before it got too loud. Usually they would make it past question 20 of the catechism before the coughing started. Today, it was at question nine.

Not that John didn't mind the break. It gave him a chance to ask a question of his own. He waited until his mother came back and sat down.

"Mother, what day did God create the seas?"

"I believe it was on the third day, John. The Bible says He gathered the waters together to form them."

"Which one is Father on right now?"

"Well . . . he sails on most of them, so I'm never quite sure. But his letter last month said they were headed to the Mediterranean."

John's father was a captain of a merchant ship and was never home very much or for very long. It had been over a year since John and his mother had seen him.

"Will Father ever take me on a sailing voyage?"

His mother smiled. "Such questions, John." She drew him close and hugged him. "Thank the Lord, He has placed your feet on dry ground. Be content to keep them there for now. Now where were we? Question ten . . ."

Thoughts of the sea were never far from John's head. It was a hard subject to avoid in a place like Wapping where they lived. Wapping was a village in England on the banks of the Thames River just outside London and was always full of sea captains, sailors and dock workers.

It was also home to the Old Gravel Lane Chapel, the church where John's mother took him every Sunday.

One Sunday instead of their regular pastor, Dr. Jennings, speaking, a visitor took the pulpit. John sat up in his pew as he listened to Dr. Isaac Watts preach. He had heard about Dr. Watts before. Their church had often sung many of the hymns he had written, including well-known ones like "When I Survey the Wondrous Cross" and "Joy to the World". But John's favorite was one Watts had written especially for children, called "I Sing the Mighty Power of God".

As he walked home from church afterwards, he held his mother's hand and sang out the words.

"I sing the mighty power of God,
that made the mountains rise,
That spread the flowing seas abroad,
and built the lofty skies . . . "

John's song was cut short as his mother began to cough again. Her coughing had become worse in the last few weeks.

When she was finally able to speak, she said, "John, I've been wanting to tell you something. I . . . I'll be going away for a while to my cousin's house by the coast. The doctor thinks the clean sea air might help my health to improve."

"Do you mean the Catletts, Mother?" John asked. "You've told me so much about them. I can't wait to visit. When do we leave?"

Tears began in the corners of his mother's eyes. "No, you don't understand, John. I'm going there. You'll be staying with the Marsden family from church."

John's mother's short visit to the coast soon turned into months.

John didn't really mind staying with the Marsdens. They were nice enough, but it wasn't the same as being at home with his mother.

One day in July, Mrs. Marsden called him from his room.

"John, there's someone here to see you."

John hurried from his room where he'd been reading. Perhaps it was his mother, or maybe his father had finally returned from a sea voyage!

Instead, John was surprised to find Dr. Jennings, their pastor. He was standing in the parlor room with a serious look on his face.

"Hello, John."

"Hello, Pastor Jennings."

"Mrs. Marsden tells me you've been busy reading this afternoon."

"Yes, sir. Dr. Watts *Short View of the Whole Scriptures*," John replied.

"That's good, John. It's an excellent read."

Dr. Jennings paused. ". . . John, I didn't come here today to talk about books, I'm afraid. I'm here to bring you some terrible news. Your mother has died."

As the tears began to stream from John's eyes, Dr. Jennings placed his hand on John's shoulder.

"John, I know you might not understand this yet, but God is full of grace and goodness even in the death of His children. All life comes from Him, and we must trust that when He takes it, it is for good, not evil."

John remained with the Marsdens through the next year until his father finally returned from his sailing voyage. At first John thought things would get better, but then his father announced that he was getting remarried and that John was going to be sent to boarding school.

Over the next several years, John hardly saw his family while he was away at school. Before long, John's father and stepmother had three children of their own. All their attention seemed to focus on these children rather than John. That was why John was surprised one day when his father made an announcement:

"You won't be returning to school this year, John. You're ten years old now and old enough to come with me on my next voyage."

A few weeks later John was boarding the ship. It seemed as if there was activity everywhere he looked: dock workers hauling barrels of supplies, sailors carrying canvas bags, officers barking orders.

Peering up at the topmast, John spied a man tying down a sail.

"Aye now. You'd better watch yourself," came a voice nearby. "Keep staring up like that and seagulls are going to mark you for an easy target."

The voice came from a young sailor perhaps three or four years older than John.

"Name's Bill. Bill Higgins. I can see from the looks of you that you ain't too familiar with this 'ere ship or any ship for that matter."

"Not really," John replied. "This is the first time my father's taken me on any of his sea voyages."

"Father? Wait now. Is yer father Captain Newton?" Bill looked a little startled. "Well I better watch me words or ye'll be sending me to the brig, right?"

John laughed. It was nice to have someone pay some attention to him for once.

"Well, come on," Bill motioned him forward. "Let me show you the rest of this 'ere ship you'll be calling home from now on."

John and Bill became good friends in no time. Although the ship was outfitted and ready for sailing, poor weather kept them from heading out to sea for several weeks. While John saw much more of his father than ever before, the captain always seemed too busy with voyage preparation to pay much attention to John's whereabouts.

One day on deck, Bill caught John's attention and whispered in his ear.

"Listen 'ere, John. I 'erd that the warship the HMS *Victory* is anchored off Purfleet down river. Now, you might think this 'ere oversized barrel is something, but you ain't seen nuttin' till you seen one of them warships with 100 guns!"

Bill glanced side to side and continued.

"Me and some of the fellers are going ashore this Sunday to see it for ourselves. How about you comin'?"

Bill whispered the details of when and where they were to meet. John knew his father wouldn't approve, but he also knew his father wouldn't notice if he was gone.

On the appointed Sunday, John slipped away after morning services. Dr. Jennings had gone on particularly long that morning, so John knew he'd have to hurry if he was going to meet Bill and the others on time.

He urged his horse on, but as he descended the hill to the wharf, he slowed up. It was too late. There were Bill and the others already paddling the longboat out toward the *Victory*.

John slid down from the saddle and bit his lip in frustration. Why couldn't they have waited just a few more minutes? Now he'd have to sit and wait to hear all about the adventure from Bill. He was sure they would joke about John's lateness too.

His grumbling was interrupted suddenly by the sound of cries!

As he looked out at the longboat, John was shocked to see the small boat suddenly lurch, then capsize. Bill and the others tumbled into the water.

He soon realized that Bill and the others were too far from land to swim and too far from the ship for help. Like most sailors, Bill and the others were not strong swimmers.

By the time a boat reached them, it was too late. They all had drowned.

A few weeks later, John stood quietly on the deck of his father's ship. The weather had cleared and they sailed out of the Thames River and entered the North Sea. As he watched the waves rolling into white crests beside the ship, the "over-sized barrel" now seemed like an "undersized cork."

John often thought about that accident. What would have happened if he'd been there and fallen in the water? He was no better at swimming than Bill.

While John didn't often think about God, this event got his attention. He knew that only God's hand of grace had kept him from reaching the longboat on time.

Surrounded by the sound of the waves, he whispered a prayer. "Lord, I . . . I don't know why you spared my life, but thank you. And from now on I promise to live a life always right and good in your sight."

But John wondered if he'd be able to keep his promise to God.

John found himself once again seated in a chair before his father's enormous desk.

"May I go now, Father?" he said while leaning forward in his chair.

"No you may not!" came the firm response. "John, I hardly know what to do with you. You've been on five voyages with me and done absolutely nothing."

John slouched back. He'd heard this before.

"I've done everything to try to make you successful like Mr. Almarez in Spain. You had a great job handling his accounts and what did you do? Walked out just because you thought it was 'too boring.' "

Now John began scuffing his feet on the desk in front of him.

"I suppose you'd rather be reading one of those books about how everything would be great if everyone could just sit around eating and drinking all the time. Well, let me tell you, son. That's not the real world. In the real world, real people work real hard for real money or they end up real poor. Do you understand!?"

John knew there'd be more unless he acted as if he was sorry.

"I'm sorry, Father. I know I've disappointed you. It's not that I don't appreciate all you've done. It's just that . . . I don't think I'm cut out to be a sea captain like you."

His father let out a sigh. "John, I don't expect you to be a captain like me. But I do expect you to prove yourself hard-working at whatever you do."

"Yes, Father. I'll try harder."

"Now then," his father continued. "I have another opportunity for you. My friend, Joseph Manesty, has offered to take you to Jamaica to help him manage his sugar plantation. If you *do* prove yourself, John, in four or five years you could find yourself very wealthy and in charge of your own plantation."

John didn't mind the thought of having plenty of money to spend.

"You sail in three weeks, John . . . *and* in case you're wondering how to spend your time before you leave, I have a job for you."

His father explained the details of a business matter he wanted John to take care of in Kent, a nearby town.

"Oh, and John, I want you to visit your mother's cousins, the Catletts, while you're out there. They've been wanting to meet you."

Two weeks later, John was on a snowy road near Kent. He'd finished the errand for his father and was eager to get on board the ship for Jamaica.

The only thing left to do was to pay a quick visit to the Catletts.

New fallen snow made it impossible for John to reach the front door without first trudging through a drift. He stomped his feet to remove the snow and gave the door knocker a sharp rap.

"Let's get this over with," he muttered under his breath.

The door was opened by a girl perhaps a few years younger than John. He had never seen anyone so beautiful.

"Hello, may I help you, sir?"

John couldn't speak for a moment. "Uh . . . yes . . . I'm John."

"John who?"

"Newton . . . John Newton."

John had never been in love before, but at the sight of this girl, he knew he was now. He soon learned that the girl was Polly, the oldest Catlett girl.

The Catletts invited John to stay with them as long as he wanted. John was happy to accept the offer, although he kept his feelings for Polly a secret. His quick visit ended up lasting three whole weeks!

John knew he'd miss the ship leaving for Jamaica and the opportunity his father had arranged, but he didn't care. He didn't want to leave England and he didn't want to be a sugar plantation owner. He wanted to be with Polly, and whatever John wanted was most important in his mind.

John's father was furious when John finally returned home. Once again he had ruined a carefully arranged opportunity. However, his father's anger soon gave way to another plan to see John succeed. This time John was to sail the Adriatic Sea with another captain, a friend of John's father. However, John would be a common sailor–no special privileges.

John set sail this time and soon learned to be an able seaman, but he also learned several sinful habits. Many of the sailors drank alcohol heavily and cursed one another and everything else. John wanted to be popular with the sailors, so he soon gave in to these temptations and joined in.

When he returned to England at the end of the year, there was only one thought on his mind: *When could he see Polly again?*

"I don't understand why you want to visit the Catletts again so soon," his father said, as John sat once more before his desk.

John didn't have an answer.

"Just make sure you're back in time to meet Mr. Daws. He's looking for a few good men to serve as officers on his ship, and I've made arrangements for you to be one of them."

"Yes, Father."

This time John hurried as fast as he could to the Catletts' house. Although he still kept his feelings for Polly secret from her and her family, there was no mistaking them in his heart. And when it was time to leave, John ignored his responsibilities. Instead he stayed with the Catletts for over a month!

Still there was one thing bothering John. He wanted to marry Polly one day, but how could he even think about it if he didn't have a job or position. Her family certainly wouldn't agree to it!

One morning in March, John traveled alone to the nearby town of Chatham. The sea air always seemed to help him think better.

As he slowly made his way down the main street, he kept thinking about his problem. "There has to be a way," he muttered to himself.

"Looks like this fella's lost," came a voice from behind him.

John turned to see not one, but three men following him.

"Seems like we might be able to help him. Don't you think, sir?"

The question was directed to the leader of the group. John could tell by the man's blue jacket that he was an officer in the British navy.

The officer gave a faint smile before speaking. "I agree. I think this gentleman might be looking for an opportunity to serve on board the *Harwich*. Isn't that right, sir?"

John realized what had happened. He'd been caught by a press gang! Press gangs were groups of men sent out by the Royal Navy to find new recruits for navy ships. They had ways of convincing whoever they found to serve. With war about to begin with France, John had picked a poor time to walk alone on the streets of a port town.

The three men led John to a building in town where he was kept under lock and key for three days while the men searched the streets for more "volunteers."

Word reached John's father about what had happened, but even his attempts to see John released ended in failure. John and the others were led on board the *Harwich* where John would serve as a seaman.

Four days after he boarded the ship, war was declared with France. Soon the *Harwich* was sailing up and down the coast providing protection for other British ships. Thanks to John's experience at sea and his father's influence, John was soon promoted to midshipman. That meant better food and treatment!

But John soon wasted the opportunity.

He treated the sailors under him with little care and was disrespectful to those in authority. One time while the ship was in port, John was given permission to go on shore for *one* day. Instead, he took *ten* days so he could visit the Catletts and see Polly again! When he finally returned, Captain Carteret was so upset that he threatened to demote John.

After his meeting with the captain, one of the officers took John aside.

"Look here, Newton. I don't think you realize just how gracious Captain Carteret has been to you."

"Yes, sir. Is that all?" John asked.

"Is that all? Is that all!? Newton, you should be grateful not to have received a good flogging!"

John remained silent.

The officer continued. "I'd advise you to change your attitude, or it's going to make the long voyage to the East Indies even more difficult for you and for us."

John looked up quickly. "What was that you said, sir? Voyage to where?"

"To the East Indies, Newton. Haven't you heard? We've been reassigned."

John couldn't believe it! The East Indies were halfway around the world! John knew that once they sailed, they would be gone from England for four, maybe five years. There would be no way to see Polly.

Throughout the next few months, John hatched a secret plan. To the surprise of everyone, it started with his being as helpful as possible. Whenever there was a task to be done, John was the first to volunteer.

One of the officers caught John's attention one morning. "I must say, Newton. Your turnaround is quite remarkable. Captain Carteret is pleased with your progress. He's even asked me to assign you to take three men and go ashore at Plymouth and get a few more supplies before we shove off."

"Yes, sir. Right away, sir." John said with a smile.

This was the opportunity he had been looking for.

John would run away. Plymouth was close enough to where his father was that he might reach him. If he pleaded with him, maybe his father would find another job for him that would allow him to be closer to Polly.

The next day John arrived on shore in the ship's longboat. While the other men loaded the boat, John disappeared in the shadows of the dock.

He quickly changed clothes and then bargained with a farmer for the use of a horse. As quickly as he could, he raced off to find his father.

At a split in the road he pulled up on the reins. *Now which way?* he thought. John wished he knew the area better. There was no time to lose. They'd be looking for him soon. He'd have to guess.

John raced down one of the roads. As he rounded the corner, he pulled up on the reins again. This time it wasn't a split in the road. It was a group of soldiers.

"Ho now!" one of them called out. "Where are you headed so quickly?"

John had to think fast. "I'm . . . heading to Exeter to find a doctor. It's my wife. She's going to have a baby!"

"Heading to Exeter, are you?" said another. "Better hurry!"

John gave a sigh of relief and began to leave.

"Except . . . you won't find it down that road," said the soldier. "Say, you wouldn't be hurrying for another reason, would you? Maybe we should have a quick look in those bags of yours."

John was captured. By nightfall he was back on board the *Harwich* under armed guard.

The next morning he was brought out before the entire crew.

Captain Carteret spoke. "Let you men bear witness that this man has deserted from His Majesty's Ship, the Harwich. In doing so he has shown disregard for His Majesty's authority and is subject to corporal punishment. Lieutenant, carry out the sentence."

John's shirt was removed and his arms lashed to an iron grating. There would be no escaping this punishment.

A cat-o'-nine tails was given by the captain to the lieutenant. John winced in pain as the lashing began.

Chapter 3
Grace Rejected

John Newton lay in his hammock in the lower deck of the *Harwich*. It had been two weeks since he had received the flogging on deck for running away. His back was red and sore and his mind was full of despair.

The ship had set sail from Plymouth, from England, and from Polly Catlett, the girl he loved. He was trapped on board, and the thought of not seeing her again for five years made John's heart sink. Even worse, no one onboard ship wanted anything to do with him. Now that he was just a common sailor, the other sailors whispered and laughed about him, remembering his proud attitude when he was an officer.

Day after day passed and John's situation went from bad to worse. One moment he was filled with anger for everybody. He even imagined murdering the captain. At another moment, John even thought of ending his own life by throwing himself overboard. Still something kept him from taking action either way.

One morning after three weeks of sailing, John awoke to the sound of supplies being loaded in the hold below him.

The *Harwich* had reached the Canary Islands off the African coast (show map) and was getting fresh food.

Although he had heard the wake-up whistle earlier, John remained in his hammock. Sleep seemed like the only place where he could escape his surroundings.

"Up on deck, Newton," said an officer as he climbed down the ladder to the lower deck.

John muttered something under his breath.

"What's that, Newton? Don't be blaming me for where you are. Now get up."

The officer followed his remark with a swift kick to the bottom of the hammock.

John snarled. "I'll get up when I'm ready to get up, and you can tell that to cap . . ."

His words were cut short by a sudden jolt. The officer had cut the rope on one end of Newton's hammock, causing him to tumble onto the floor.

"There, now get up on deck as I said!" shouted the officer.

Newton scrambled up from the floor and thought about carrying out his plans of murder on the officer rather than on the captain, but all he could say was, "All right, I'm up."

When John finally emerged onto the deck he noticed some unusual activity. Another sailor was loading his belongings onto a longboat.

"Where's he going?" John asked a sailor nearby.

"He's being traded for a sailor from a merchant ship. I hear they're looking to trade one more."

A thought quickly went through John's head. Anyplace would be better than here.

John hurried over to a nearby lieutenant.

"Beg your pardon, sir," he began, acting as respectful as possible. "I'd like to volunteer to be the other man traded off this ship."

The officer sneered back, "I hardly think that anyone would want you, Newton. We'd probably have to pay them to take you . . . still, it would be nice to be rid of you. Wait here."

John watched as the lieutenant talked with Captain Carteret and the captain of the merchant ship. Finally he returned to John.

"All right, Newton, pack your bag. You've just been dismissed from His Majesty's Service.

Within a half hour, John had packed his bags and climbed on board the *Pegasus*, a merchant ship captained by a man named Penrose. The captain greeted John.

"I hear yer last name is Newton. Ye wouldn't be any relation to Captain John Newton from Wapping, would ye?"

"He's my father," John replied.

"Well then," the captain continued. "I welcome you on board as the son of a dear friend. I'm honored to have you join us. My first mate, Mr. Blunt, will show you your quarters."

John followed Mr. Blunt, but as they descended below deck the first mate paused for a moment.

"Mr. Newton, I want to make you aware that I do not share Captain Penrose's enthusiasm for having you aboard. Any man unfit for the Royal Navy is unfit for this ship . . . but I hope you prove me wrong."

John Newton did not prove Mr. Blunt wrong.

In the weeks that followed, John became well known on board the *Pegasus* for his laziness. He also used every opportunity he could to curse and swear as a way to impress his fellow sailors.

His actions certainly didn't impress Captain Penrose, but the captain put up with John's attitude even after John made up a song for the crew that made fun of the captain!

All that changed later in the year though when Captain Penrose suddenly became sick and died. A new captain was named–Mr. Blunt.

John knew that, as soon as he was able, Captain Blunt would trade John back to a navy ship as a common sailor. John had to get off the ship quickly.

There was a man traveling aboard the *Pegasus* by the name of Amos Clow. John had heard Clow tell stories about the "factory" he operated on the African coast. This factory was not a place where things were made, but instead a terrible place where African slaves were kept in chains until they could be loaded on ships and sold on the other side of the ocean. What really got John's attention was Clow's stories about the money that could be made. John thought about all he could do if only he had plenty of money. Maybe he could even get back to England and marry Polly!

Clow agreed to take John on as a business partner and Captain Blunt gladly agreed to let John go.

John was so glad to leave that he didn't even ask for his pay. *I'll have plenty of money of my own soon enough*, he thought.

It didn't take long for John's dreams to disappear.

Before he could even start working with Clow to get slaves, John got very sick. Instead he had to stay at Clow's home while Clow traveled upriver.

"My woman Pi will take care of you," Clow said as he left.

John soon found out that Pi had no interest in taking care of him. Instead, she treated him like one of her slaves, giving him only a little water and a few leftovers from her meals.

His condition quickly got worse. One day he was so weak from fever that after begging for some food, he dropped his small plate of food in front of Pi.

"Is that how you respond to my kindness?" she cried out in front of all her servants. "Then you shall have no food at all!"

That night John was so hungry, he climbed out the window of his room into the moonlit yard. His stomach twisted in pain as he desperately searched for anything to eat.

There! He spied some cassava plants growing nearby. The roots were often boiled up for food. John clawed them out of the ground with his fingers and tried to eat them raw. The uncooked roots soon caused John to throw up.

No doubt, John would have died from illness and starvation were it not for the kindness of others. Pi's other slaves began to sneak food to John so he could get better. They also secretly carried letters John wrote in desperation to his father asking for help.

When Clow finally returned, John complained to him about his treatment, but Clow wouldn't listen, especially with Pi standing nearby.

John was glad that when it was time for the next business trip, as he was well enough to go with Clow. But after a trader falsely accused John of stealing, Clow began to treat John like a slave too!

John was chained on board the small riverboat. His only food and water came from the fish he caught and the daily rain showers.

John continued to be treated as a slave by Clow and Pi to the point that he began to lose his mind. But just when he was losing hope of ever being free they decided to trade John to another factory owner in the area. This man, instead of keeping John in slavery, fed and clothed him and paid him for his work. Soon John was not only healthy again, but he was even given ownership over part of a factory.

John quickly forgot his days as a slave or how it felt to be treated as one. Now that he had some money and power, he decided to live his life exactly as he wanted to, eating and drinking and using his position to treat his slaves harshly and to force them to do whatever he wanted. He even began to learn about the false gods of the natives and began to take part in their strange and ungodly rituals. It seemed that John could go no farther away from God.

Little did he know there was a plan to rescue him.

Back in England, John's father had not forgotten about his son. He had received the letters John had sent while a slave of Clow and Pi. Despite all of John's past failures, his father still pitied him. He learned of a ship named the *Greyhound* that was heading to the African coast where John was located. Captain Swanwick had orders to try to find John and rescue him, if possible.

One warm February day John was resting on the front porch of his home when he heard men approaching. It was one of his business partners accompanied by three other men.

"There he is. That's John Newton," said his partner pointing to John.

John sat up expecting to make a deal to sell some slaves.

"John Newton," began Captain Swanwick, "I've been looking for you."

"For me? What for?" John wondered if he owed the man some money.

"Your father sent me to rescue you and bring you home to England on board my ship."

John paused for a moment. He remembered the letters he'd sent. But now as he looked around at his house and thought of the money he was making, he laughed.

"Rescue? I think you can see that I'm not in need of any rescue. Tell my father that I don't need him."

With that John stood up and rather rudely began to make his way inside.

"Hold there a minute, Newton. Don't you realize how fortunate you are that I even found you? I was about to sail by this bit of land except that I saw your friend here signal for trading."

John laughed again. "Well then, I guess you're the lucky one. Go ahead and trade. I'm going inside."

Captain Swanwick wasn't about to give up.

"Before you go, Newton, there's something you ought to know. Your father wanted me to tell you that you've come into a sizable inheritance. It seems an aunt of yours has passed away and left her fortune to you!"

"What was that?" asked John, turning from the door.

"You've inherited a fortune! I've been instructed to bring you home. You'll be my personal guest on board the *Greyhound*."

Within an hour John had packed up his belongings and left his African home. It was too good to be true. He was to be wealthy beyond his dreams! Even wealthy enough to marry Polly Catlett.

In reality it *was* too good to be true. Captain Swanwick had made up the story and it had worked. John was now a passenger on board the *Greyhound*.

It didn't take long for Captain Swanwick to wonder why he had gone to all this trouble to rescue John. As a passenger, John had no responsibility on board. Instead he passed the time with drinking and cursing. As John told the stories of his past adventures to the crew, Captain Swanwick's opinion of John worsened.

"I'm no saint myself, Mr. Newton, but if there ever was a Jonah, it's you," he said half-jokingly one day as they dined. "I'm afraid no good will come to us for taking such a rebel as you on board the *Greyhound*."

John thought little of Captain Swanwick or his words.

After finishing their trading along the African coast, the *Greyhound* made its long journey toward England by making a big circle following the trade winds out in the Atlantic.

To pass the boredom of the long trip out at sea, John turned from drinking to reading. One night he read a book that talked about living a life completely devoted to God and the peace and joy it brought. The more John read, the more he was reminded of his own life and his attempts to find satisfaction in all the world had to offer.

In the stillness of the cabin, he mused, *What if these things are true?* He quickly pushed the thought from his mind, closed the book and went to sleep.

In the middle of the night John suddenly awoke to the thunderous sound of waves and a cry from deck, "The ship is sinking!"

The *Greyhound* had been trapped by a huge storm in the North Atlantic. As water began to pour into his cabin, John jumped to his feet and began to climb the ladder to the deck.

"Newton!" the captain shouted. "Get my knife from the cabin!"

John turned back on the ladder and let another crew member pass. Then in horror he watched as that man emerged on the deck and in the next instant was swept overboard to his death. Except for the captain's command, Newton would have been the one caught in the wave!

John's narrow escape seemed only temporary as the whole ship was battered by wave after wave. One section of the bow was destroyed and water flooded in. The crew and John pumped and bailed hour after hour as more water flooded in.

As the captain looked at their hopeless situation he turned to John.

"Did I not say you were a Jonah! We'll no doubt all die unless we throw you overboard!"

Still the crew continued to battle the storm into the morning hours. Although the winds had let up a little, there seemed little doubt the ship would sink.

"Grab any wood you can to patch that hole," cried the captain to the crew. Then turning to John he said, "It's our only hope."

John could only answer, "If it won't do, then may the Lord have mercy on us!"

Chapter 4
Grace Received

John Newton feared for his life. He and the other crew members of the *Greyhound* were in the midst of a North Atlantic gale that had already swept one man overboard to his death. All John could do was cry out, "May the Lord have mercy on us."

It was the first time John had ever called on God in real fear and respect, but he was afraid it was too late.

Although the storm winds had started to die down a little, the damage had already been done. There was a huge hole in the ship's bow and water was gushing in at several places. It seemed only a matter of time before they would all meet a watery grave.

All day long the crew pumped and bailed water in desperation, while the captain tried to steer the ship with its tattered sails.

As night approached, all were exhausted.

"Newton," the captain called. "You've been at sea more than most of my crew. Take the helm and steer if you want to live."

As John piloted the ship through the night he kept thinking, *What mercy can there be for me? I've cursed the name of the Lord and refused His grace again and again. Surely, this is the punishment I deserve!*

Still the ship stayed afloat. But even then the men realized they were still in danger. Almost all of their food had been washed overboard, and it would take weeks to reach land with their ship in its current condition.

Day after day passed with no sight of land on the horizon, but John began to find hope somewhere else. One item that had survived the storm was a Bible. When John wasn't busy pumping, bailing or steering, he began to read it.

In the book of Luke he read of the prodigal son, the story of a young man who had wasted all his father had given him and lived just as he pleased. That reminded John of himself. Yet, in the story, the young man returned home and found his father with open arms, rejoicing and willing to receive him. That was God and His grace, or at least that's what John hoped.

After almost four weeks at sea, the cry finally came, "Land ho!"

The *Greyhound* limped into the harbor at Lough Swilly in the north of Ireland. They had survived.

As John placed his feet on dry ground, tears began to stream down his cheeks. He cried out, "Thank you, Lord. You have heard the prayer of this wretched sinner and You have answered it in Your grace."

God had saved him from the storm. John now knew he could trust this same God to save him from his sin.

At first John acted like a completely different person. Instead of going to the local tavern in Londonderry, he started going to church—every day, twice a day! He stopped cursing too!

John did his best to act as a Christian should, but soon found it was hard, if not impossible, to live this way for very long! The temptation to sin was too strong.

John had been saved by grace, but God was teaching him that he must live by God's grace, too.

Two months later John finally arrived back in Liverpool, England. He had written his father and hoped to find him there, but he was a couple days too late. His father had already set sail on a voyage to Canada. It wasn't the only disappointment either. John soon found out that Captain Swanwick's story about his inheriting a fortune was nothing but a trick to get him on board the ship. Now John was without a job, without any money, and without any hope of ever marrying Polly Catlett.

John knew this was what he deserved too. Rather than lead Polly on any further, John decided to write her family and tell them that he would quietly disappear from Polly's life just as if he had sunk to the bottom of the sea.

But the letter he received back from Polly's aunt brightened his hopes. She said that before John's father had sailed, he had visited the Catletts and that the two families had agreed that John and Polly should be married . . . if Polly agreed.

Still, John had no job. How could he possibly ask her to marry him?

John was walking the streets of Liverpool one afternoon when a man approached him.

"Are you John Newton?"

"Yes."

"My master, Joseph Manesty, wants to see you."

Joseph Manesty? John remembered how as a young man he had once rejected Manesty's offer to work his sugar plantation. What did Joseph Manesty want with him now?

Within an hour John stood in Manesty's office.

"Welcome, John!" Manesty said as John entered. "I've been looking for you. Captain Swanwick works for me. He gave me his report of the *Greyhound* and of the storm. He told me about your help in steering the ship and of your changed attitude afterward."

"Yes, sir," John answered.

"John, I need a man like you to captain my ship, the Brownlow. How about it?"

John couldn't believe Manesty would offer him, of all people, a position of such importance!

"Thank you, sir. I know I don't deserve such a position—in fact, I'm not sure I'm ready yet."

Manesty rubbed his chin for a moment.

"You may be right, Newton. I appreciate your honesty. What about serving as first mate? If you prove yourself, there will be a captaincy waiting in your future."

John agreed.

The *Brownlow* was different from the other ships John had been on before. It was a slave ship headed for the coast of Africa. There it would pick up a load of slaves and bring them across the Atlantic Ocean to be sold in the Americas. The *Brownlow* wasn't the only slave ship either. In those days there were hundreds of other ships doing the same thing. As a young Christian, John hardly thought about the evils of the slave trade or of getting involved in it.

Throughout the voyage of the *Brownlow* a war was going on within John's heart. John was now a Christian, but he still enjoyed some of his old ways of living too. Although he didn't curse anymore, he continued to do what he wanted especially when it to came to how he treated the slaves. After dropping off the slaves, the *Brownlow* stayed in Charleston, South Carolina, for several weeks before making the trip back to England. The war in John's heart continued. During the day he would find a quiet place to spend time with the Lord through Bible reading and prayer, but then at night he'd spend time in a tavern surrounded by others who drank and cursed.

As they sailed back toward England, John had even more time to read the Bible. Little by little he began to follow God and to turn from his old ways.

When they arrived back in England, the *Brownlow's* captain gave Joseph Manesty a good report about John's work.

Once again, John was called to Manesty's office.

"John, I'd like to offer you the captaincy of my ship, the *Duke of Argyle*," Manesty said. "You'll set sail next summer."

A captain! John was again overwhelmed by the offer and by God's grace to him. But would God show him grace in one other way?

John traveled the same road to the Catlett's house that he'd once taken as a young man. When he arrived, Polly met him at the door. She was just as beautiful as the day they'd first met.

After dinner with the family, John and Polly sat together in the parlor room.

John knew what he wanted to say, but his tongue seemed twisted in his mouth and sweat was pouring down his forehead.

After several moments of silence, Polly finally reached over and took his hand and simply said, "Yes, John."

Two months later John and Polly were married.

The next few months seemed like a dream for John. He wished he could spend every day with Polly for the rest of his life, but he knew summer was coming and so was his first voyage as a sea captain.

In August 1750, the *Duke of Argyle* set sail from England. Like the *Brownlow*, the *Duke of Argyle* was a slave ship. While John was growing in grace, he still didn't see the wickedness of the slave trade—not yet.

Over the next four years, John captained the *Duke of Argyle* and another ship called the *African* through three voyages. There were many dangers along the way. One time slaves tried to take over the ship. Another time it was mutinous sailors. Once, slaves attempted to poison the ship's water supply. Disease claimed the lives of many slaves, sailors and others, including one of John's close friends.

Then John received the terrible news that his father had drowned in an accident during the voyage to Canada. Sadness and regret filled John's heart, knowing that he'd never see his father face-to-face to ask forgiveness for his past.

Even though John was now a captain, during the long ocean crossings he actually had quite a bit of free time. He wrote many letters to Polly, read many books and even taught himself the ancient languages of the Bible. More importantly, John continued to spend time with God through reading the Bible and praying. Little by little John was changing.

He no longer drank, and began to treat his sailors and even the slaves better. He started to gather the crew on Sundays for simple church services that he would lead. This became one of John's favorite things to do.

Near the end of his third voyage as a captain, John met a merchant ship captain named Alexander Clunie. Clunie wasn't a typical captain. He was a Christian and attended a church back in England similar to the one John had attended with his mother.

The two men became close friends and began to study the Scriptures together each evening while in port. This was another gift of God's grace. John needed a Christian friend like Clunie to help him understand God's Word and to encourage him to live each day trusting in the Lord for help.

Back in England, John sat one morning with Polly at tea. He only had two days left at home before he was to set sail again.

"John, must you leave again so soon?" Polly asked. "It seems like you just got here."

"I'm afraid so, dear," John replied. "Mr. Manesty has his new ship called the *Bee* sitting in Liverpool Harbor waiting for me to captain."

Polly smiled. "I seem to remember a young man who used to keep Mr. Manesty waiting."

John laughed. "That was when I was young and foolish and in love. And now? Now, I love you even more, but I'm older and hopefully a little wiser." He paused for a moment. "Still I wish I could stay. Not just because of you either. It's this slave ship business. Sometimes I feel as if I'm a jailer on a floating prison. There's something not right about it, but what can I do?"

John took a sip from his teacup. Suddenly, he began to feel a tingly feeling in his head. The room began to spin around him and the cup fell from his hand.

"John!" Polly shouted. "What's wrong!?"

As much as John wanted to answer, his whole body seemed unable to do anything. He tumbled to the floor.

When John finally awoke, he found himself in bed. Polly was standing at one side and the doctor on the other.

"What happened?" he mumbled.

"We're not sure, Mr. Newton, but you've had quite a fall," said the doctor. "And you've given your wife and everyone else quite a scare. It will take several weeks before you're up and about again."

"Weeks?" John said as he began to try sitting up. "What about the *Bee*? I'm supposed to sail in two days!"

"I don't think you'll be sailing anywhere anytime soon," the doctor responded.

Polly brushed a wisp of hair from John's eyes. "I guess Mr. Manesty will have to wait after all."

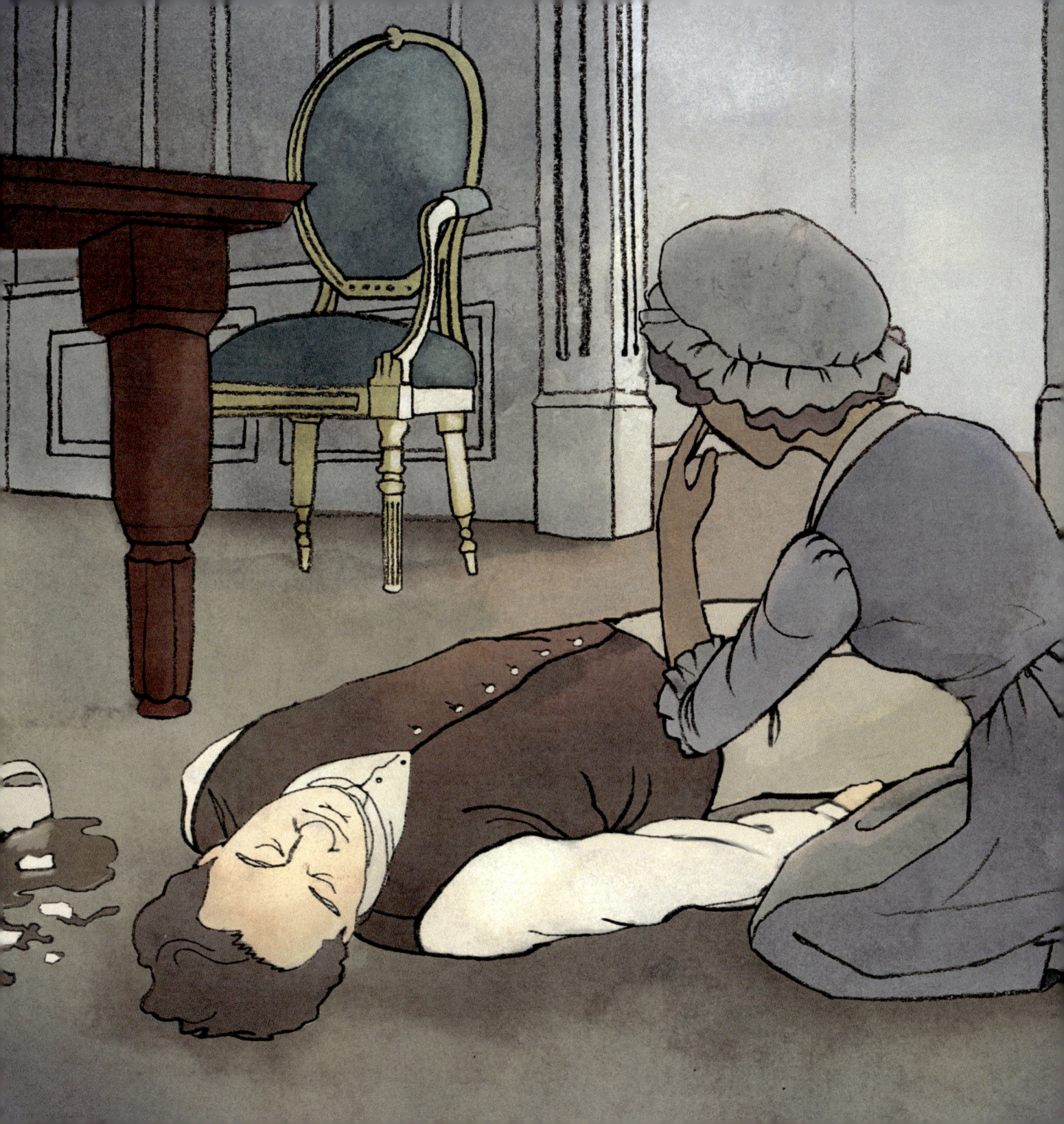

Over the next few months, John's health slowly returned. His illness was never explained, but it turned out to be a blessing. The Bee set sail without John and he was just as glad. Now he had a reason to leave slave trading and to be with Polly more.

There was only one problem. John didn't have a job or any way to support his wife!

But again, God provided. Joseph Manesty helped John become the Surveyor of Tides for the city of Liverpool. John's job was to examine ships as they came into harbor and to make sure they paid the correct amount of money to the government for the things they carried.

While the job kept John, at times he had so much free time. Instead of wasting it as he had in the past, John began to take an even deeper interest in the things of God. His friend, Alexander Clunie, had recommended several churches in the area, and John made it a point to attend them and to listen to the preaching of God's Word.

Not all the preaching was inside of church buildings either. One day a famous preacher named George Whitefield came to Liverpool for several outdoor meetings. Whitefield stood at a pulpit set up in an open area and preached for all to hear. John listened as Whitefield, with his booming voice, spoke from Isaiah 25:4:

> "For thou hast been a strength to the poor,
> a strength to the needy in his distress,
> a refuge from the storm . . ."

John remembered how the Lord had saved him from the storm and had given him grace to turn from his sinful ways over the past years. But as he looked at the crowd gathered, there were young and old, rich and poor. They all needed to know God in the same way. They needed more preachers like Whitefield who would faithfully tell them of God's grace.

Who would tell them?

"Well . . . that's the end of that, Polly. I'll never be a preacher."

John and Polly sat in the back of a coach. They were returning to Liverpool after a visit to a church in Leeds where John had been asked to speak for the first time.

"John," Polly began as she took hold of his hand. "it wasn't as bad as you think. You just got a little tongue-tied."

"Tongue-tied? Polly, it was an absolute disaster. I couldn't remember anything I planned on saying. All I could do was stand there speechless and shake like a leaf in front of all those people."

Polly did her best to encourage him. "Perhaps next time you should write your sermon down first."

"Next time?" John shook his head. "No . . . I think I should probably give it up and stick to my job in Liverpool."

"John, you know you're not happy there . . . and think of all you've done already to prepare yourself to be a minister in the Church of England."

Over the past several years, John had studied hard on his own. While he'd never gone to college, he'd taught himself through reading book after book and learning the ancient languages the Bible was written in originally.

Back in his study that night, John bowed his head in prayer.

"Lord, you know how unfit I am to be a minister for You. But if You want me to, I'm willing, Lord. Please give me grace to know and to do Your will."

John prayed this way day after day.

After 42 days, he had peace that it was God's will.

However, others weren't so sure. Several other ministers refused to approve John as a minister. Some said he didn't have the education while others thought he spent too much time with "radicals" like George Whitefield and the Wesley brothers.

Again John began to doubt God's leading and wondered if he should become a preacher outside of the Church of England. But Polly was there again to encourage him.

"If this is God's will, John, He'll work it out in His way. Just wait and see."

"Perhaps you're right, Polly. Maybe the Lord is using all this to teach me patience and humility. Or maybe it's to help me realize what a treasure I have in a wife like you."

Polly smiled. "We can talk about that later. Right now there's a man waiting in the study to see you, John. He says his name is Thomas Haweis."

John had never met Mr. Haweis before, but he soon found out that Mr. Haweis knew quite a bit about him.

"Mr. Newton, a friend of yours shared with me some of the details of God's work in your life. I must say, it's a remarkable story."

"Well, Mr. Haweis, there's much there that I am not proud of, but if it has been used to show God's grace and to bring Him glory, then I'm glad to have the story told."

"That's exactly my point, Mr. Newton. I think that many others would be encouraged in their faith if they could hear this story too. That's why I'd like to ask your permission to publish it in a book."

John was unsure at first, but he finally agreed. Over the next few months, he wrote down his story in letters to Mr. Haweis. Before long they were published in a book called *An Authentic Narrative*. The book became very popular as people read of Newton's adventures and of God's grace to him. Soon people all over England knew the name "John Newton."

One of those who read the book was Lord Dartmouth, an important nobleman who controlled large amounts of land in England. Within his land a place called Olney needed a minister. Lord Dartmouth recommended John for the position.

Still there were some in the church who were against it, but Lord Dartmouth didn't give up. He wrote several letters and arranged a meeting between John and an important church leader. Finally, John was accepted. On April 29, 1764, after six years of disappointments and waiting, John became a minister of the Church of England.

"Now the real challenge begins," he told Polly.

"What do you mean, John?"

"To preach what I should and to live what I preach."

Olney had only 2,000 people in it, most of them poor cottage workers, but John determined to serve faithfully where God had led him.

Each Sunday he would preach once in the morning and once in the afternoon. In the evenings he'd lead a smaller Bible study. Throughout his sermons, John would often share some of his life story. His example was a great encouragement to those who thought their own sins were too great to receive God's grace.

But John wasn't content to simply preach God's grace from the pulpit. There were other opportunities to proclaim it.

"Polly, I have an idea," John said one day. "You know that big mansion Lord Dartmouth owns behind the church?"

"You mean the one that just sits there empty?"

"Yes. It would be perfect for children!"

"John! You know that God hasn't allowed us to have any children."

"That's not what I mean, Polly. I mean that it'd be a perfect place for us to have a children's meeting during the week. After all, the children of Olney need to hear of God's grace too!"

Within a few weeks, the first children's meeting was held in the house. Eighty-nine children showed up the first night! Forty-four more came the next week! John told them Bible stories, taught them hymns and shared about his own life.

When John wasn't leading services or meetings, he was often found wearing his old seaman's jacket, visiting the people of Olney. He'd spend time listening to them, giving them godly counsel and praying with them, especially in times of need.

One day John's travels took him beyond Olney to a village where another minister lived. John thought this might be a good opportunity to finally meet the man, but as he was led inside the home by a servant, he realized something was wrong.

In the parlor stood an older woman and a younger man both dressed in black.

The woman stepped forward. "Reverend Newton, we have heard so much about you and your work in Olney. My husband, Reverend Unwin, would have greatly enjoyed meeting you . . . but I'm afraid . . ."

Tears welled up in her eyes.

"I'm afraid you've come to us at a time of great tragedy. My husband died two days ago after falling from his horse. We are in mourning. This young man with me is Mr. William Cowper. He has lived with my husband and me for several years and has been like a son to us. He shares in my great sadness."

John had expected to make only a short visit, but now seeing Mrs. Unwin and Mr. Cowper, he stayed for several days to comfort them.

Later, when a new minister was assigned to replace Reverend Unwin, John and Polly opened up their home to Mrs. Unwin and William.

Mrs. Unwin became a great help in the children's meetings by leading the music. While Mr. Cowper was much quieter, he and John became close friends. John soon found out that William was a wonderful poet.

As the two were walking one day in the garden, John spoke up. "William, I've always found that the children seem to understand and remember God's Word so much better when they have a hymn to help them. I think that the same is true with adults. Would you consider using your skill with words to write some new hymns?"

Mr. Cowper looked up nervously. "I . . . I'm not sure I'd know how to go about it, Mr. Newton."

"Well, perhaps we could work on them together. You look over my work and I'll look over yours."

Through John's encouragement, William wrote many hymns, including ones still sung today, like "There is a Fountain Filled With Blood." Along with John's hymns, William's works were eventually put together in a hymnbook called the *Olney Hymns.*

As the year 1772 ended, John thought back on God's grace in his own life. God had brought him through many dangers including the depths of his own sin. God had blessed him with a loving wife and given him the opportunity to proclaim the Word of God as a minister. With thankfulness in his heart, John wrote the words to a new hymn to be used at the New Year's Day service. It began,

> Amazing grace! how sweet the sound,
> That saved a wretch like me!
> I once was lost but now am found,
> Was blind, but now I see.

Little did John think that this hymn would become so well known and much beloved. By singing its simple words, many have joined their voices in proclaiming God's grace.

But two years later John wasn't thinking about many people. He was thinking about one person in particular.

"What will become of dear Betsy?" asked Polly between sobs.

They had just received a letter saying that Polly's brother had died. His wife had already died from illness which meant that their five-year-old daughter, Betsy, was now without anyone to care for her.

"Well," John said, "Isn't it ob-vious what will become of her? She'll come to live here, of course. I might be almost 50, but I'm not too old to be a father."

Betsy wasn't the only family member that John and Polly took into their home. Polly's aging father lived with them until he passed away and another niece named Elizabeth moved in after both of her parents died from tuberculosis. The Newtons loved both Betsy and Elizabeth as daughters, but they were especially concerned for Elizabeth.

"Elizabeth's getting worse," Polly said one night. "She was coughing all day."

John nodded. "I know . . ."

"Oh John, do you think it's tuberculosis?"

"I think so, Polly. We'll do everything we can to care for her, but that must not be our only concern. She needs Christ in her heart. We must pray that the Lord will speak to her through His Word and show her that need. If she trusts Christ, it won't matter if she dies at age 12 or 112. She will be forever with our Saviour."

Over the next two years, John and Polly gave Elizabeth the best medical care for her illness, but John also spent each morning and evening teaching Elizabeth the Bible and praying with her.

In October 1785, Elizabeth passed away. While John and Polly were very sad, they also rejoiced. Before dying, Elizabeth had put her faith in Christ.

Over the years another important change happened in the Newtons' lives. John had left Olney in 1780 to become the minister at a church in London called St. Mary Woolnoth. Unlike in Olney, John's new ministry was in the middle of a city full of activity and important leaders.

One evening a young man came to their house for a private meeting with John. His name was William Wilberforce. Wilberforce was a member of the British Parliament that governed the country. Like Newton, he had once been a rebel living a sin-filled life, but now he had trusted in Christ.

"Mr. Newton. It seems like politics is such an ugly business. People are always lying and looking for ways to gain more power for their own selfish purposes. Do you suppose it's any place for me?"

John knew the importance of godly leaders.

"My prayer for you, William, is that God will make you a blessing both as a Christian and as a statesman."

John had no idea just how important his advice would be.

Wilberforce continued to serve in politics and eventually became the leader of a movement to get rid of the slave trade in the whole British Empire. It was a hard battle. Many powerful leaders fought against him because slavery brought lots of money into the country.

By now, John himself had realized the sinfulness of slavery. He now began to work with Wilberforce to show the people the great sin of the nation.

John had a powerful tool to help convince others—his own experiences. He wrote a small book about the horrors of the slave trade. As many read it, they too began to support the end of slavery.

In the middle of John's ministries, Polly's health worsened, especially after she developed a cancerous tumor. While it was very hard for John to see Polly in pain, God continued to give grace to him and to Polly even to the end. As John sat by her bed on a December night in 1790 he thought back to that December night in 1742 when he had first seen her beautiful face.

"Lord," he prayed, "may I ever rejoice in You even if You take my dear Polly."

By the end of the night, Polly was gone. God answered John's prayer by giving him strength a few days later to preach at Polly's funeral.

For the next 16 years, John continued to serve as minister at St. Mary Woolnoth. Finally, old age and memory loss forced John to step down. His adopted daughter Betsy was now married and she and her husband helped take care of John.

In February 1807, John heard the good news. William Wilberforce had been successful. The slave trade was finally outlawed in the British Empire.

Near the end of the year, an old friend stopped by to visit John, who was now so weak he had to stay in bed. With a whisper he said, "My memory is nearly gone, but I remember two things: That I am a great sinner and that Christ is a great Saviour."

A few days later John died at the age of 82. Yet, even in death John continued to proclaim God's grace through the story of his life and through the hymns he wrote that are still sung today.

One hymn called "Glorious Things of Thee Are Spoken" proclaims:

Grace which, like the Lord, the Giver,
never fails from age to age.

John had known the great depths of God's grace. And God in His love continues to offer that same grace to all who will call upon Him for salvation. His grace is amazing!

We then, as workers together with Him, beseech you also that ye receive not the grace of God in vain... behold, now is the accepted time; behold, now is the day of salvation.

2 Corinthians 6:1, 2

Chapter 1

1. What did John's mother teach him as a young boy? *(The Westminster Shorter Catechism; questions and answers about God)*

2. Why did John not see his father very often? *(His father was a merchant captain and was often away at sea.)*

3. Who was the guest speaker John heard at his church? *(Isaac Watts)*

4. Name one of the hymns written by Isaac Watts. *("When I Survey the Wondrous Cross," "Joy to the World," "I Sing the Mighty Power of God")*

5. Why did John's mother go away when he was young? *(She was very sick and needed fresh sea air.)*

6. Where was John sent after his father returned from the sea? *(To boarding school)*

7. What did John and his friend plan to go see? *(A British warship on the river)*

8. How did God show grace to John by allowing him to arrive late to meet his friends? *(John avoided being drowned when the ship overturned.)*

Chapter 2

1. Who was upset with John at the beginning of the chapter? Why?*(His father; John had been lazy)*

2. Why did John miss the ship heading to Jamaica? *(He fell in love with Polly and didn't want to end his visit with her family.)*

3. What happened to John while he was walking the streets of Chatham? *(He was captured by a press gang and forced to serve in the Royal Navy.)*

4. How did John treat the other sailors on board the *Harwich*? *(He was mean to those under him and disrespectful of those in authority.)*

5. What did John do when he was allowed one day to go on shore? *(He took ten days to visit Polly.)*

6. Why did John decide to desert the Royal Navy? *(He knew the ship was going to sail for the East Indies and that he wouldn't be able to see Polly.)*

7. How was John punished for deserting? *(He was flogged in front of the other sailors.)*

8. How did John respond to God's grace throughout this chapter? *(He continually ignored God's grace and wasted opportunities.)*

Chapter 3

1. Why was John full of despair on board the *Harwich*? *(No one wanted anything to do with him; he was far away from Polly)*

2. How did John get off the Royal Navy ship? *(He was traded for a sailor on a merchant ship.)*

3. What was a factory? *(A place where slaves were held before they were sent on ships to the Americas)*

4. What did John do to make fun of Captain Penrose? *(He wrote a song.)*

5. What did Pi do when John dropped his plate of food? *(She forced him to go without any food.)*

6. When John became part owner of a factory, how did he treat the slaves? *(He was unkind and did whatever he wanted with them.)*

7. How did Captain Swanwick get John aboard the *Greyhound*? *(He told John that he had inherited a fortune from an aunt.)*

8. How did God show grace to John in the middle of the storm? *(John just missed being swept overboard when he went to get a knife.)*

Chapter 4

1. What story in the book of Luke helped to give John Newton hope? *(The Prodigal Son)*

2. What changes in his life did John make immediately after surviving the storm? *(He went to church every day and stopped cursing.)*

3. Why did he struggle to resist the temptation to sin? *(He needed to depend more on God's grace every day.)*

4. What job did Joseph Manesty offer John? *(Captain of a slave ship)*

5. How did Polly show John she accepted his proposal of marriage? *(She just took his hand and said "yes.")*

6. Name some ways that John was growing in grace even while a slave ship captain? *(He was spending more time in God's Word, he treated the sailors and slaves better, he started holding Sunday services on the ship.)*

7. What happened that allowed John to get out of the slave ship business? *(His unexplained illness caused him to miss the ship's sailing.)*

8. What famous preacher did John hear in Liverpool? *(George Whitefield)*

Chapter 5

1. Why did John think about giving up becoming a minister? *(He would forget what he was going to say; others opposed him becoming a minister.)*

2. How did John Newton become well-known all over England? *(Through people reading his book,* An Authentic Narrative*)*

3. What was the name of the place where John first ministered? *(Olney Parish)*

4. What did John and Polly do with the mansion behind the church? *(They hosted children's meetings.)*

5. What did John encourage William Cowper to do? *(To write hymns)*

6. What famous hymn did John Newton write for a New Year's Day sermon? *("Amazing Grace")*

7. How did John and Polly help to care for their niece Elizabeth? *(They gave her medical care; John spent time teaching her God's Word.)*

8. Before John died, what was outlawed in the British Empire? *(Slavery)*

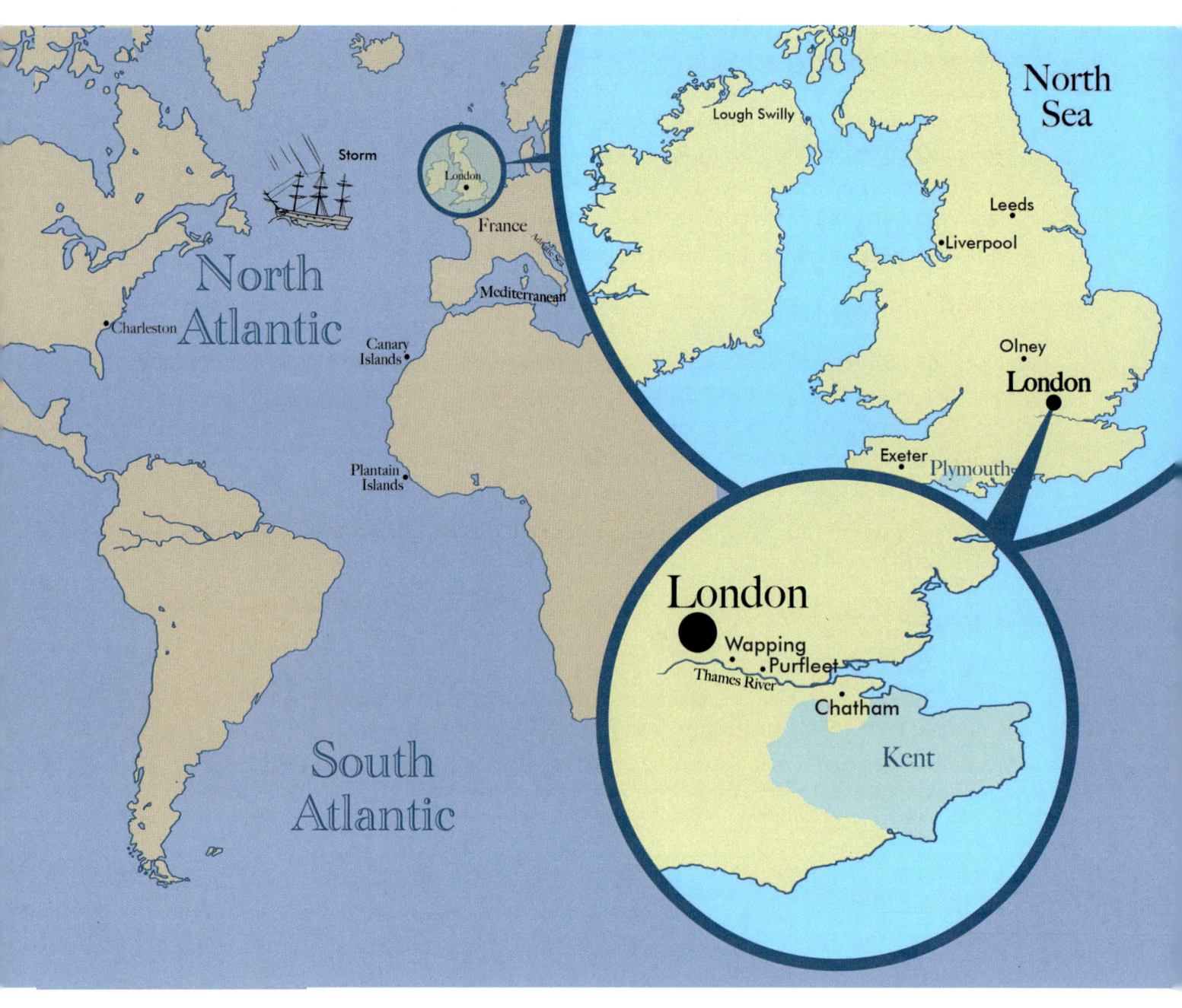

Storm

North
Atlantic

•Charleston

Canary
Islands •

Plantain
Islands •

South
Atlantic

France

Mediterranean

Adriatic Sea

London

North
Sea

Lough Swilly

Leeds •
•Liverpool

Olney
•

London
•

Exeter
•   Plymouth

London

● •Wapping
       •Purfleet
Thames River

•Chatham

Kent